W9-DIZ-475

SCOTT SNYDER
Writer

JOCK
FRANCESCO FRANCAVILLA
Artists

DAVID BARON
FRANCESCO FRANCAVILLA
Colorists

JARED K. FLETCHER
SAL CIPRIANO
Letterers

JOCK
Collection Cover

BATMAN CREATED BY BOB KANE

THE BLACK MIRROR

Mike Marts
Editor – Original Series

Janelle Asselin
Associate Editor – Original Series

Katie Kubert
Assistant Editor – Original Series

Peter Hamboussi
Editor

Ian Sattler
Director – Editorial, Special Projects and
Archival Editions

Robbin Brosterman
Design Director – Books

Eddie Berganza
Executive Editor

Bob Harras
VP – Editor in Chief

Diane Nelson
President

Dan DiDio and **Jim Lee**
Co-Publishers

Geoff Johns
Chief Creative Officer

John Rood
Executive VP – Sales, Marketing and
Business Development

Amy Genkins
Senior VP – Business and Legal Affairs

Nairi Gardiner
Senior VP – Finance

Jeff Boison
VP – Publishing Operations

Mark Chiarello
VP – Art Direction and Design

John Cunningham
VP – Marketing

Terri Cunningham
VP – Talent Relations and Services

Alison Gill
Senior VP – Manufacturing and Operations

David Hyde
VP – Publicity

Hank Kanalz
Senior VP – Digital

Jay Kogan
VP – Business and Legal Affairs, Publishing

Jack Mahan
VP – Business Affairs, Talent

Nick Napolitano
VP – Manufacturing Administration

Sue Pohja
VP – Book Sales

Courtney Simmons
Senior VP – Publicity

Bob Wayne
Senior VP – Sales

BATMAN: THE BLACK MIRROR

Published by DC Comics. Cover and
compilation Copyright © 2011
DC Comics. All Rights Reserved.

Originally published in single magazine
form in DETECTIVE COMICS 871-881
© 2011 DC Comics. All Rights Reserved.
All characters, their distinctive likenesses
and related elements featured in this
publication are trademarks of DC Comics.
The stories, characters and incidents
featured in this publication are entirely
fictional. DC Comics does not read or
accept unsolicited submissions of ideas,
stories or artwork.

DC Comics, 1700 Broadway,
New York, NY 10019
A Warner Bros. Entertainment Company
Printed by RR Donnelley, Salem, VA,
USA. 1/13/12. Second Printing.
ISBN: 978-1-4012-3206-1
SC ISBN: 978-1-4012-3207-8

SUSTAINABLE
FORESTRY
INITIATIVE
Certified Chain of Custody
Promoting Sustainable
Forest Management

Fiber used in this product line meets the
sourcing requirements of the SFI program.
www.sfiprogram.org SGS-SFI/COC-US10/81072

STORY SO FAR

In the aftermath of the universe-shattering events
known as the Final Crisis, Gotham City's Dark Knight
was presumed dead.

With the mantle of the Bat unclaimed and the city
unprotected, original Robin Dick Grayson took up the
cape and cowl as Gotham's new Batman, joined by
Bruce Wayne's son Damian as Robin. The two formed a
new and decidedly different dynamic duo, while former
sidekick Tim Drake assumed the identity Red Robin.

But when a very much alive Bruce Wayne reappears,
he does not immediately return to his old role as
Gotham's Caped Crusader. Instead, the original
Dark Knight sets out on a larger mission: Batman,
Incorporated. Recruiting allies around the world,
Bruce forms a franchise of Batmen to protect the
entire globe.

And the burden of protecting Gotham City is once
again left on the shoulders of protégé Dick Grayson...

the black mirror

When I was a boy, my parents kept a *big map* of the country tacked to the wall of our dressing room.

The map had pins stuck in all the places our troupe was going to stop that season.

Different towns and cities were marked with different color pins.

Blue pins meant small towns...which meant small shows, less dangerous tricks.

Red pins meant big cities. So, big shows and more dangerous tricks.

All the stops were marked red or blue...

POOL

...except for one-- *Gotham City*, which was marked by a *black pin*.

The lab was Tim's idea, of course.

He figured that with Wayne Industries offering funding to Batman, it'd be a slap in the face to the G.C.P.D. not to extend help to the department, too.

So after Bruce's return, Wayne Industries opened a new, state-of-the-art forensic lab, and made the facility available to the G.C.P.D., free of charge.

GOOD TO SEE YOU AGAIN, COMMISSIONER. SO WHAT DO YOU THINK?

WELL, IT'S CERTAINLY SHINY, MR. GRAYSON.

CALL ME DICK, PLEASE. YOU DROVE ME TO MY HIGH SCHOOL PROM.

ACTUALLY I DROVE MY *DAUGHTER* TO HER HIGH SCHOOL PROM. YOU JUST HAPPENED TO BE IN THE *CAR.*

FAIR ENOUGH. HOW CAN I HELP, COMMISSIONER?

I TAKE IT YOU HEARD ABOUT THE INCIDENT AT GOTHAM PREP YESTERDAY?

THE POOL ATTACK? JUST WHAT WAS IN THE PAPERS.

That was nearly seven weeks ago. And the G.C.P.D. still hasn't sent a single evidence bag our way...until today.

So, my question is-- why now?

THE TWELVE-YEAR-OLD BOY WHO ATTACKED THE OTHERS-- DANA REDFORD. WE FOUND *THIS* IN HIS LOCKER. IT'S A HORMONAL MUTAGEN. CAUSES WHAT'S KNOWN AS RAPID, ATAVISTIC REGRESSION.

A KIND OF REVERSE EVOLUTION. WE FIRST ENCOUNTERED THE STUFF A FEW YEARS AGO, WHEN IT WAS GIVEN TO--

KILLER CROC... I REMEMBER READING ABOUT IT IN THE BLUDHAVEN P.D. FILES. TOOK A GUY WITH A SKIN CONDITION AND BAD TEETH, TURNED HIM INTO A GENUINE MONSTER.

BATMAN *in*
DETECTIVE
COMICS

THE BLACK MIRROR
part TWO of THREE

SCOTT SNYDER *writer*
JOCK *artist & cover*

DAVID BARON *colors*
JARED K. FLETCHER *letters*

The man in the car is **William Rhodes.**

CFO of Rhodes Metals, the country's largest producer of high-grade titanium alloys. His product is used in everything from high-speed magnetic trains to orthopedic joints.

Hero to local charities. Socialite. In short, one of Gotham's golden sons. Until **three hours ago,** that is...

...when Oracle connected him to a secret society called **"Mirror House,"** an organization that auctions off illegal material that once belonged to Gotham's most notorious villains.

Now William Rhodes is a wanted man. And I've got **questions** for him.

...AND...DONE. WILLIAM RHODES IS NOW ALIVE AND WELL, AND ABOUT TO USE HIS CREDIT CARD TO BUY A VINTAGE OF OUR CHOOSING FROM WEST GOTHAM WINES.

ANY RECOMMENDATIONS FOR HIM?

YOU KNOW MY TASTE.

ON SECOND THOUGHT, I'LL CHOOSE. ANY WORD ON THE REDFORD BOY?

SAME. THE REDFORDS MADE THEIR MONEY IN IMPORTS.

MY GUESS? ONE OF THEM FELL IN WITH THIS *"DEALER"* GUY, LET HIM USE THE FAMILY NAME AND EQUIPMENT TO MOVE AUCTION GOODS.

UNTIL THEY DECIDED NOT TO ANYMORE.

AND THE DEALER DIDN'T LIKE THAT. HENCE THE MAD HATTER TAG.

POOR KID DANA PROBABLY STUMBLED ONTO A STASH BEING KEPT AT HIS HOME FOR AUCTION AT MIRROR HOUSE.

FAMILY BUSINESS.

ABOUT THIS MIRROR HOUSE... I COMBED THE ARCHIVES, CAME UP WITH NOTHING. STILL, THE NAME RANG A BELL.

SO I STARTED ASKING AROUND, TALKING TO SOME OF MY OLD HIGHER-UPS, RETIRED GUYS FROM WAY BACK.

TURNS OUT A COUPLE OF THEM REMEMBER HEARING RUMORS ABOUT SOME PLACE, AN *UNDER-GROUND AUCTION HOUSE* DEVOTED TO BADDIES.

SUPPOSEDLY THEY MOVE AROUND, HOLD THEIR LITTLE GET-TOGETHERS AT SITES WHERE NASTY THINGS WENT DOWN. CULT TYPE THING.

FUNNY THING IS... THESE GUYS, THEY SAY THEY REMEMBER HEARING MENTION OF IT WAY BACK... TEN, TWENTY YEARS AGO.

SEEMS MIRROR HOUSE HAS BEEN OPEN FOR BUSINESS IN GOTHAM A *LONG TIME.*

NOT JUST IN GOTHAM.

This neighborhood, Gramercy Row, used to be a nice place to live.

The **earthquake** hit it hard, but still, if you'd told me back then that this was what it'd look like today, I would have laughed in your face.

Maybe Barbara is right. Maybe it's the circus blood, but I've lived in Gotham most of my life, and still, I've never gotten over how fast the city can **change.**

How fast it can turn into a **stranger** right before your eyes...

HOW'S THE NEW FACE?

IT TICKLES.

NO PROBLEMS, THOUGH?

WHY, TIM?

I RAN AN S.A.T. SCAN, JUST AS AN AFTERTHOUGHT, AND THERE'S A BLACKOUT FIELD IN EFFECT.

MEANING YOU WON'T BE ABLE TO COMMUNICATE WITH ANYONE FROM INSIDE. NO PHONE, NOTHING.

BATMAN in DETECTIVE COMICS

SCOTT SNYDER *writer*
JOCK *artist & cover*

DAVID BARON *colors*
JARED K. FLETCHER *letters*

THE BLACK MIRROR
part THREE of THREE

My family had three rules for staying alive on the trapeze. The first was: *"Pick a point."*

Meaning, pick the point in space you're headed for and never look away, even for a second...

Etienne Guiborg. Commonly known as **The Dealer**. He runs underground auctions for wealthy Gothamites, auctions devoted to the worship of the city's worst elements.

FRIENDS, I LEAVE MY BELOVED GOTHAM IN THE MORNING. PLEASE, MAKE THIS A NIGHT I CAN SAVOR IN MEMORY UNTIL MY NEXT VISIT!

NOW, TAKE HIM!

THEN THERE IS NO TIME.

GUIBORG SAID HE WAS LEAVING TOWN IN THE MORNING. THAT MEANS RIGHT NOW.

I NEED TO GET TO THE BUNKER. IF WE PULL UP-- AGGH!

REST IS WHAT YOU NEED. YOU'RE BEATEN TO A PULP. AND THE GAS--

I CAN HANDLE IT. JUST HELP ME ACCESS THE CHARTER WING OF GOTHAM INTERNATIONAL AIRPORT. I CAN DO IT, BUT YOU CAN DO IT FASTER.

IF HE'S LEAVING, HE'S PROBABLY USING THE REDFORD FAMILY PLANE. IT'S A PRIVATE CARGO.

DICK, WE HAVE A BEAD ON THE MONEY. I'M DIGGING IN DEEPER EVERY DAY, EVERY HOUR.

IN A WEEK, WE'LL BE ABLE TO GET THIS GUY WHENEVER AND WHEREVER WE WANT. THERE'S NO RUSH.

NO.

HE NEEDS TO GO DOWN HERE...

"THESE, THEY'RE JUST SOME OLD THINGS I FOUND LYING AROUND..."

JUST TOSS IT IN THE RIVER.

AS YOU WISH, SIR.

I'LL TELL YOU, ALFRED, THIS CITY...JUST WHEN YOU THINK YOU'VE SEEN EVERYTHING IT HAS TO THROW AT YOU...

I MEAN, YOU EXPECT THAT KIND OF VICIOUSNESS FROM THE ARKHAM CROWD. BUT THOSE PEOPLE AT MIRROR HOUSE. JUST PLAIN CITIZENS. MOTHERS AND FATHERS...

LATELY IT JUST FEELS LIKE THE CITY IS GETTING MEANER, WILDER. SOMETHING IS CHANGING. SOME NIGHTS I FEEL LIKE I BARELY RECOGNIZE IT ANYMORE.

MAY I REMIND YOU HOW LITTLE SLEEP YOU'VE BEEN GETTING? I TOOK IT UPON MYSELF TO HAVE THE MATTRESS CHANGED AGAIN. SHALL I WAKE YOU FOR A LATE SUPPER, MASTER RICHARD?

MASTER RICHARD?

These are the questions I get asked the most by people around Gotham...

...and these are my answers.

"You ever shot anyone?" And my answer is, "Too many times."

"You ever been shot?" And my answer is, "Too many times."

And the question I get the most... "How do you leave it all behind when you go home?" My answer to this one is: "You learn to block it out."

But that's not the truth.

The real truth is that when you've been doing this as long as I have--you don't leave it behind. You can't.

Because no matter how good you think you are at drawing a line between work and home, there will always be some cases that stay with you...

...cases that come howling back at you out of the darkness, like phone calls in the middle of the night.

IT'S BLOOD, DAD. I KILLED A WAITRESS WHILE YOU WERE TALKING TO BARBARA. HER HEAD IS STUFFED IN THE TOILET OF THE MEN'S ROOM.

IT'S JUST KETCHUP, SEE?

I'M SORRY.

I WAS TRYING TO MAKE A JOKE...I'M NOT GOOD AT HUMOR. THAT'S PART OF IT. I'M SORRY.

TWO MINUTES. THEN I'M GONE.

Something
I can fend off...

See through it.
Your mind is a shark.
A shark swim--

COMinG...

COMinG...

To

EAT You...

No...that can't...

Eat you uP DICKiE!!!

EAT You!

EAT You!

EATYOU!!!

The Peter Pan case. Fifteen years ago, over the course of eight months, eight children went missing from their beds.

Eventually, one by one, their bodies turned up in the city dump. They'd been drugged unconscious with *ether...* mutilated.

As a cop, I deal with the human capacity for evil every day.

It's a fact. It exists in people. People like *Roy Blount.*

You might not see it at first glance. Because on the surface, he's just a quiet man who owns a small cleaning business.

Sure, he did some time at Blackgate for *arson,* but he was just a stupid kid playing with matches. He didn't mean to set that fire.

Hell, no one was even hurt, except him. Burned up his whole left side. Either way, look at him, he paid his dues. He's just trying to get his life back on track is all. He's an earnest, stand-up guy.

But look closer, look right when I tell you, and you'll see it too, the *real* Roy beneath the surface.

He has been out of jail a week, and I've watched him every night.

Because when you've been a cop as long as I have, you get good at seeing it in people, that *dark spark* of something... something beneath.

WOW! ƎHAHAƐ THOSE ARE SOME SERIOUS SPACE GOGGLES. SUN HITS THEM THE WRONG WAY AND YOU COULD FRY SOMEONE. BE CAREFUL!

EXCUSE ME?

DON'T LISTEN TO HER. SHE'S JUST TEASING YOU.

OH. I GET IT. BECAUSE OF MY GLASSES. MEANING, THE LENSES COULD FOCUS THE SUNLIGHT TO CREATE A HOTSPOT. THAT'S... FUNNY.

YOU WERE ASKING ABOUT THIS, THOUGH...

IT'S A *SCIENCE KIT*. BESS AND I BOUGHT IT TOGETHER A COUPLE YEARS AGO. WE SHARE IT. I KEEP THE BOX, SHE KEEPS THE KEY. SO WE CAN ONLY USE IT WHEN WE'RE TOGETHER.

VOILA.

CAN I SEE IT?

SURE, IT'S HEAVY THOUGH. HERE.

SO, TELL ME ABOUT THE *OLDER BOYS*, BABS.

TELL YOU WHAT?

OH COME ON, YOU SKIP TWO GRADES AND...WHAT THE--

WHAT THE HELL ARE YOU *DOING?*

HE ALMOST BROKE THE LOCK. LOOK AT THIS! YOU LITTLE TWERP.

WHY WOULD YOU DO THAT, JAMES?

I WAS TRYING TO OPEN IT FOR YOU, BARBARA. BUT THE LOCK IS TRICKY.

BUT... WHO SAID I WANTED IT OPENED?

I'M SORRY. I JUST FIGURED, THAT WAY, IF BESS EVER *WENT AWAY,* YOU'D STILL BE ABLE TO USE IT YOURSELF.

WENT AWAY? WHAT ARE YOU TALKING ABOUT?

WHY WOULD SHE EVER GO AWAY, JAMES?

I MEANT *MOVED* AWAY. WHAT IF HER FAMILY MOVED SOMEDAY.

¿UGH¿ COME ON, BABS...LET'S GO.

JEEZ, AND I THOUGHT *MY* BROTHER WAS CREEPY.

YOU CAN PLAY WITH THEM IF YOU WANT, JAMES.

THAT'S OKAY, MRS. GORDON. I CAN MAKE MY OWN FUN.

There. There it is. You see it? He's going to kill someone tonight.

There in Roy's eyes.

To everyone else, he's just a man walking down a snowy alley.

But you saw it. It's all still there **underneath**.

The **real** Roy beneath this one. The predator. The killer.

No, that Roy, the one beneath, he hasn't gone anywhere...

ANYTHING?

NOT YET. THE OTHERS ARE STILL LOOKING.

JIM? WE'RE DOUBLING BACK. OVER.

GOT IT. WE SHOULD HAVE MORE EYES UP HERE ANY MINUTE. OVER.

TELL HIM, HONEY.

TELL ME WHAT?

I SAW SOMETHING IN JAMES'S HAND, DAD.

THERE WAS SOMETHING IN IT, AND I THINK IT WAS BESS'S KEYCHAIN.

HER KEYCHAIN? WHAT ARE YOU SAYING, BARBARA?

I'M SAYING...

...I THINK HE *DID* SOME-THING TO HER, DADDY...

*...I THINK IT WAS **HIM**."*

You scratch the surface and the evidence is there. It adds up. Like with Roy.

See, before he caused that mysterious fire, he already had a record as a sex offender.

His weren't big offenses, nothing huge. But all of them involved children.

Still, all that got hidden during Roy's time in Blackgate. Because by a glitch, his record as a sex offender was allowed to expire during his incarceration.

Look deeper and you'll find another clue: because that burn on old Roy's arm and neck, it's a **flash burn**.

YOU KNOW, I USED TO READ **PETER PAN** TO MY DAUGHTER WHEN SHE WAS A LITTLE GIRL. YOU REMEMBER HOW IT ENDS, ROY? I'LL TELL YOU...

...PETER PAN, HE COMES BACK TO WENDY'S HOUSE AFTER ALL THOSE YEARS...

The kind of thing that happens when a highly combustible fluid ignites. Like **ether**. Like if you had ether on you, and you were smoking a cigarette, and you weren't careful...

...you'd go up like a flare, and then you'd get caught, and then you'd get sent away.

And see, then, if someone like me, if they happened to notice that right around the time you got sent away, the Peter Pan killings stopped... they'd find another clue, Roy.

...AND HE FINDS THE WINDOW LOCKED.

Because with a little cross-referencing, they'd see that all the families with kids that disappeared, all of them used your cleaning business at one time or another.

And if you, Roy, cleaned their houses, then it'd stand to reason you'd have ample opportunity to leave the door unlatched or make a key to fit... if you wanted. And then, Roy...

...YOU'RE... YOU'RE JIM GORDON.

SUPER-COP, *HEH.* YOU WERE ALWAYS RIGHT BEHIND ME.

SWING YOURSELF TOWARD THE LEDGE, BLOUNT! I CAN'T HOLD YOU.

YOU WANT A CONFESSION, GORDON?

ONE DAY BACK THEN, I DECIDED HELL, YOU WERE OUT TO GET ME, WHY NOT COME AFTER YOU, TOO?

SO THE SUMMER BEFORE MY ACCIDENT, I *DID* COME AFTER YOU...

...I FOLLOWED YOU UP TO THAT SUMMER HOUSE OF YOURS...

...AND I CAME FOR YOUR BOY...

"...TELL ME THE *TRUTH!*"

SO ONE DAY ≿COUGH≾...I WAITED OUTSIDE 'TIL YOUR OLD LADY LEFT JAMES ALONE FOR A SECOND...

...AND I WALKED UP TO HIM, AND I HAD A WHOLE STORY CONCOCTED, HOW I WAS LOST, HOW I HAD TOYS IN MY CAR...

TELL ME THE TRUTH, DAMMIT!

"...HE LOOKED UP AT ME. AND..."

...HE SMILED AND HE SAID, "I KNOW WHO YOU ARE"...AND THE LOOK HE GAVE ME, IT SENT CHILLS UP MY BACK. *ME...*

YOU'RE LYING...

LET GO, JIM!

IT WAS *YOU,* WASN'T IT, ROY?! *YOU KILLED BESS!* YOU!

LET GO, COMMISSIONER.

"AND I DON'T KNOW WHO YOU WERE EXPECTING TO SEE OPEN THOSE *BIRD CAGES,* BUT IT WAS JUST A COUPLE SKATER PUNKS. COULDN'T HAVE BEEN MORE THAN THIRTEEN YEARS OLD..."

"SO IS THAT GOOD NEWS, COMMISSIONER?"

"FUNNY THING IS, I'M NOT SURE ANYMORE."

"IS ANY OF THIS PART OF SOMETHING I SHOULD KNOW ABOUT?"

"JUST AN OLD CASE..."

"...SOMETHING THAT DIGS AT ME, ON NIGHTS LIKE THESE."

LOST BOYS

SCOTT SNYDER writer

FRANCESCO FRANCAVILLA artist

JARED K. FLETCHER letters

"*GOTHAM GLOBAL MODERN BANK* OCCUPIES THE FIRST SEVEN FLOORS OF THE HISTORIC BEACON BUILDING ON THE CITY'S EAST SIDE.

"FOUNDED JUST SIX YEARS AGO, G.G.M. IS NOW ONE OF THE CITY'S FASTEST GROWING AND MOST PROFITABLE BANKS.

"ALL IN ALL, IT'S A LITTLE *POWERHOUSE* OF A PLACE.

"THREE-HUNDRED-AND-ELEVEN BILLION IN ASSETS. 12.2 BILLION IN EQUITY ALONE.

"IT'S GOT A GOOD REPUTATION AMONG ITS EMPLOYEES, TOO. OFFICIALLY, G.G.M. OPENS AT 8 AM.

"BUT MOST OF ITS PEOPLE ARE OUT FRONT BY 5 AM, WHEN THE BUILDING DOORS UNLOCK. TO GET AN *EARLY START* ON THE DAY.

"WHAT THEY FOUND IN THE LOBBY OF G.G.M. THIS MORNING, THOUGH..."

"A PLACE LIKE THAT MUST HAVE EYES ON THE FLOOR."

"PLENTY. BUT ALL THE CAMERAS ARE LOOPED TO A MAIN SERVER."

"AND WHAT, SOMEONE RAN A *BLINDFOLD?*"

"SEEMS THAT WAY. THE SERVER WENT DEAD FOR ALMOST AN HOUR LAST NIGHT, BETWEEN FOUR AND FIVE IN THE MORNING."

HUNGRY CITY

PART ONE OF THREE
SCOTT SNYDER: WRITER
JOCK: ARTIST & COVER
DAVID BARON: COLORS
SAL CIPRIANO: LETTERS

ZUCCO.

AS IN ANTHONY "FATS" ZUCCO. THE MAN WHO KILLED YOUR PARENTS.

WOW...

-:*SIGH*:- WELL, AT LEAST WE KNOW WHERE TO START DIGGING.

THAT'S THE THING. WE HAVE DUG. AND SONIA SEEMS CLEAN.

SEEMS?

IS. FAR AS WE CAN TELL.

SO TONY ZUCCO HAD A KID.

WHAT DO WE KNOW ABOUT THE MOM--

--OTHER THAN THAT SHE WAS BLIND, OBVIOUSLY?

...

IT'S MY SON. HE'S BACK IN GOTHAM.

JAMES?

HE SAYS...HE CLAIMS TO BE *DIFFERENT* NOW.

HE'S ON MEDICATION. SOMETHING CALLED DIAXAMYNE. IT'S NEW. I DID SOME CHECKING THOUGH, AND I SUPPOSE IT SEEMS ON THE LEVEL. I...I DON'T KNOW.

I WAS HOPING YOU MIGHT MEET WITH HIM.

ME?

I CAN'T...I CAN'T SEE THIS ONE CLEARLY, DICK. I'M TRYING TO, BUT...WHEN IT'S THIS CLOSE...

OF COURSE I'LL DO IT, COMMISSIONER. JUST SAY WHEN.

PROMISE ME SOMETHING, DICK.

PROMISE ME YOU'LL BE *HONEST* WITH ME. I NEED TO KNOW.

YOU SEE SOMEONE NEW, SOMEONE GOOD-- FINE. BUT YOU SEE SOMETHING ELSE--

RIIIPPP

...before I come back down to earth.

Sonia Branch, born Sonia Zucco, daughter of Tony Zucco, the man who **murdered my parents.**

It turns out the girl inside the whale was her personal assistant. A young woman by the name of Evelyn Marr.

By all accounts, Sonia and Evelyn were close. Girlhood friends.

The coroner's report suggests that Evelyn died inside the whale's stomach. Meaning she was **eaten alive.**

HELLO? IS SOMEONE THERE?

MS. BRANCH.

BATMAN? WHY... WHY ARE YOU HERE?

TO HELP FIND EVELYN'S KILLER.

CAN I SPEAK WITH YOU FOR A MINUTE?

NO. NO YOU *CAN'T.* PLEASE... I ALREADY TOLD THE POLICE-- I DON'T KNOW ANYTHING.

SHE LEFT WORK ON FRIDAY AND THAT WAS THE LAST I SAW OF HER. I THOUGHT SHE WAS VISITING HER MOTHER... HER MOTHER'S IN THE HOSPITAL...

...OH GOD, EVELYN... *SNIFF*

I CAN'T...

SONIA. *TALK* TO ME.

PLEASE, YOU HAVE TO *LEAVE.* I HAVE OTHER PEOPLE CLOSE TO ME, PEOPLE THEY'LL COME AFTER--

WHO? WHO WILL COME AFTER--

I CAN'T... I CAN'T.

CLICK

"JUST STOP THIS. STOP *HURTING* PEOPLE.

"*PLEASE...*"

Sonia Zucco--daughter of Tony Zucco, a known dirtbag and murderer. A lowlife thug for the Maroni Family.

ACING...TRACING...
ACING...TRACING...
650560450-004450-045011550-00408-00-0
650560450-004450-045011550-00408-00-0
2650560450-004450-045011550-00408-00-0
2650560450-004450-045011550-00408-00-0
2650560450-004450-045011550-00408-00-0
2650560450-004450-045011550-00408-00-0
TRACING...TRACING...

020254065

ADDRESS ACQUIRED
0559000-0066-005
1700 00BW-GOTH

ADDRESS ACQUIRED

Sonia Branch--upstanding citizen. Gotham success story. Innocent victim...

...and there goes Gotham again... shifting right beneath my feet.

The number Sonia called belongs to a man named **Bixby Rhodes.**

He runs an extremely high-end car dealership here on the northern tip of Gotham.

He sells some of the most expensive cars in the world, customized to be even **more** expensive.

Cars with carbon fiber bodies, computerized windshields, diamond dust paint and 1,200 horsepower.

Word on the street is that in just the last year, he's become one of the city's premier gun smugglers.

He hides clients' weapons in custom-ordered luxury cars. The prize at the bottom of the cereal box.

He's a new guy, a new face on the street-- to me at least.

Question is, how and why is he involved with Sonia Branch?

The man who just tried to kill me--*Bixby Rhodes*--is a high-end weapons smuggler.

Moves guns in and out of Gotham in luxury cars. His associates call him the "*Roadrunner.*"

Hey, if the shoe fits...

And now his lunch is *pissed.*

UNNNH!

CRAAASH

...I STILL REMEMBER THE MORNING IT HAPPENED...IT WAS A TUESDAY. SUNNY OUT.

I WAS JUST ROLLING UP IN MY WHEELCHAIR TO THIS GEM, A 1979 SKYHAWK, BLACK AS NIGHT WITH CHROME TRIM.

I HAD THE GOODS IN MY HAND AND I WAS JUST ABOUT TO PUT THEM IN THE TRUNK...

...AND THEN... *WHOOSH!* BEFORE I KNEW WHAT HAPPENED, I WAS A THOUSAND FEET ABOVE THE CITY.

THE BIG BLUE BOY-SCOUT.

"SON," HE SAID, WITH THE CLOUDS DRIFTING BY BELOW US, "YOU DON'T WANT TO GO DOWN THS ROAD. TRUST ME."

THING IS, I COULDN'T GET OVER HOW *FAST* IT'D HAPPENED. IT PUT THE FEAR OF GOD IN ME. RIGHT THEN I SWORE, I'D NEVER GO BACK TO METROPOLIS. NOT EVEN FOR A *DAY.*

SONIA B--

SONIA BRANCH. I KNOW.

BUT SEE, THAT'S WHAT I'M TRYING TO *TELL* YOU. METROPOLIS IS A CITY WHERE *GODS* WALK THE STREETS.

BUT *GOTHAM?* IT'S A CITY OF *MEN.* AND UNDER THAT MASK, YOU'RE JUST A *MAN.* SAME AS *ME.*

WHICH IS ALL ONE WAY OF SAYING, HEH, HEH...I AIN'T TELLING YOU--

CRUNCH

AAARGH!

WHOOPS. MY BAD.

YOU WERE SAYING?

YOU FREAK! I'LL KILL YOU! YOU BUSTED MY LEG! YOU--

OH NO. WHAT A KLUTZ I AM. HERE, LET ME HELP YOU UP.

WHAT--YOU GOT NOTHING ON ME! *NOTHING!* WHERE ARE YOU TAKING ME?

OH, I THOUGHT I COULD SHOW YOU MY CAR AND SEE IF THERE'S ANYTHING YOU THINK I COULD DO TO MAKE IT A LITTLE *SWEETER*...

...YOU BEING SUCH AN *AFICIONADO* AND ALL...

"HE HAS YOU, YOU KNOW..."

I spent most of last night running tests on tissue samples.

The whale had deep abrasions along its belly, heavy scraping from when it'd been dragged into Gotham.

The abrasions were full of iron oxide, sessilia, and methane. Meaning rust, barnacles and natural gas.

All of which leads me to believe that Tiger Shark is likely using the old gas pipeline to move material in and out of Gotham.

Bingo. Definitely tampered with, and not too long ago, either.

So now that I've found Tiger Shark's front door, all that's left to do...

There are two kinds of performers in a circus. The "seasonals" and the "lifers." The seasonals come and go. The lifers are all in, **always.**

My parents were lifers. Lifers stuck with other lifers. We sat together in the dining tent, watched each other's kids...

...one man I remember watching me a number of times was a high-diver named Francis Roy.

His stage name was the **"Dive Bomber,"** and in his act, he would climb to the top of an eighty-foot tower, and then dive off...

...plunging into a tank of water less than **three feet deep.**

It was mesmerizing to watch. I remember one time, when he was babysitting me, I asked him what the trick was, how he dived into such a shallow tank without breaking his neck?

And he said to me, "Dickie boy, it's all about **judgment.** Early judgment.

"Meaning, you have to judge the situation right away, **from the diving board.** Before you jump. Not from the air, but from the board."

I think it's fair to say that on this one, I missed the diving board altogether.

The man in the mask calls himself **Tiger Shark.**

He's a pirate, a high-end trafficker of material in and out of Gotham City.

He's wanted for the murder of a young woman named **Evelyn Marr,** assistant to banker **Sonia Branch.**

Evelyn was found in the belly of a whale just like the one below me. **Eaten alive.**

My assumption was that Tiger Shark killed Evelyn to intimidate Sonia into laundering money for him.

But I'm starting to think that maybe, he killed her just for **fun.**

TIGER SHARK WILL ASK YOU ONE LAST TIME, BATMAN.

WHAT WERE YOU DOING SO FAR FROM SHORE, IN *HIS* WATERS?

PRACTICING MY BACKSTROKE. NOW ASK TIGER SHARK WHY HE *KILLED* EVELYN MARR?

HEH HEH...

TIGER SHARK SAYS, TODAY, MANY PEOPLE THINK THAT THE ACT OF FORCING SOMEONE TO *"WALK THE PLANK"* IS A MYTH. BUT IN TRUTH, IT WAS A VERY *REAL TRADITION* DURING THE GOLDEN AGE OF PIRACY IN THE 17TH CENTURY.

IN FACT, THERE WERE SOME CAPTAINS WHO MADE SUCH FREQUENT USE OF THE ACT THAT SHARKS WOULD FOLLOW THEIR SHIPS FOR *THOUSANDS* OF MILES, WAITING FOR THE MOMENT SOME POOR FELLOW WOULD BE FORCED OFF INTO THE BLUE.

THE MORE VICIOUS PIRATE CAPTAINS WOULD EVEN *TEASE* THE SHARKS ON OCCASION, BY FORCING ONE OF THEIR OWN CREW OFF THE BOAT IN ADVANCE OF THE REAL VICTIM, JUST TO WHET THE SHARKS' APPETITE...

...SOME OLD OR SICKLY MEMBER OF--

NO!

AAAIIEE!

DO YOU SEE TIGER SHARK'S TIE? IT'S MELANISTIC JAGUAR. DO YOU SEE HIS SHOES? KING COBRA. HIS SUIT? MADE FROM THE BACKS OF ANGEL SHARKS.

HE WEARS CLOTHING MADE FROM ONLY THE RAREST, MOST "ENDANGERED," OF NATURE'S CREATURES.

WHY, YOU ASK HIM, BATMAN? BECAUSE WHILE YOU CALL TIGER SHARK A PIRATE, A SMUGGLER, HE IS, IN TRUTH, PART OF A PROUD LINEAGE--

-- THE SEA PEOPLE OF ANTIQUITY...

...THERE IS A RECORD OF US AS EARLY AS THE TEMPLES OF RAMESES II, IN THE SECOND MILLENNIUM B.C..

COME HERE, SAYS TIGER SHARK, BATMAN. COME HERE AND SEE.

WE HAVE BEEN RESPONSIBLE FOR THE CULTIVATION--AND THE DESTRUCTION-- OF SOME OF HISTORY'S GRANDEST CIVILIZATIONS. HITTITE, MYCENAEAN, MITANNI...

"...WE ARE BRINGERS OF LUXURY, BATMAN, OF CULTURE AND LANGUAGE, OF FOLKLORE AND *MYTH*. WE SAIL WITH THE TIDES, FOR WE ARE THE CHILDREN OF THE SEA."

LOOK, LOOK UPON HIM!

He booby-trapped the yacht.

Of course he did. I want to say I saw it coming. I want to say something witty, but all I can think is...

...well played, sir.

Because with a blast hole that big, the ship will take less than a **minute** to flood.

And worse, the tide of water will be pushing into the vessel, so it'll be near **impossible** for a man caught inside to fight his way out through the current.

But even if he was able to escape, he'd be nearly 1,000 feet beneath the surface of the ocean by my best estimate.

And at that depth, the pressure would be nearly **unbearable** for him.

Besides, even if his suit were equipped to withstand the pressure, he'd still have to be able to hold his breath long enough to reach the surface.

A feat that'd take even a great swimmer roughly... seven minutes? Which would be near impossible for anyone.

Well... except, maybe, someone who's downright overcautious (or who's been **trained** to be overcautious) when it comes to seafaring missions...

...and so makes sure to boost his oxygen levels by ingesting significant amounts of pure O_2 in advance.

If the guy in question--if he was that **crazy**, maybe--just maybe--he'd squeak by?

BATMAN! BATMAN, IS THAT YOU? WE'VE GOT A SIGNAL FROM YOU AGAIN.

AHOY.

PHEW. AND YOU'RE ALL RIGHT?

REPORTS OF MY DEATH →KOFF KOFF←...I'M FINE. JUST **HURRY**...

"...I HAVE AN IMPORTANT APPOINTMENT TO KEEP."

JAMES?

JAMES GORDON? IS THAT YOU?

HELLO, DICK.

I HARDLY KNOW HOW TO RESPOND TO THAT, BATMAN.

AFTER ALL, ROADRUNNER AND TIGER SHARK, THEY'RE NOT THE CRIMINALS OF OLD. I'D HAVE TO BE PRETTY *CUNNING* TO OUTDO THEM.

DON'T SELL YOURSELF SHORT.

ALL RIGHT, SUPPOSING-- AND JUST SUPPOSING--I DID USE YOU TO TAKE THEM BOTH DOWN, WOULD THAT BE *SO WRONG?*

THEY WERE HARASSING ME TO LAUNDER MONEY FOR THEM. THEY *KILLED MY FRIEND.*

YOU'D BE GUILTY OF OBSTRUCTING THE LAW.

HA! THE *LAW?* YOU'RE GOING TO STAND THERE, TRESPASSING ON MY PROPERTY, IN A MASK AND CAPE, AND TALK TO ME ABOUT THE *LAW?*

MAN, I NEED A DRINK.

YOU TAMPERED WITH EVIDENCE AND REDIRECTED THE INVESTIGATION. IT'S ARGUABLE THAT HER KILLER, TIGER SHARK, ESCAPED BECAUSE YOU WASTED TIME BY SENDING ME AFTER RHODES FIRST.

TRUE. THEN AGAIN, IT'S ARGUABLE THAT HER KILLER, TIGER SHARK, ESCAPED BECAUSE *YOU* FAILED TO CATCH HIM--ISN'T IT BATMAN?

...judge it from the diving board, high above, before you're falling...before you're in danger.

That's what Francis Roy used to say. I can still picture his act, too. Picture him up there, standing at the top of his tower, so high above the crowd, above us all...

...looking down at the water, assessing the drop.

It's funny to think that no one knew that that's where the **real feat** happened--in that quiet moment before, not the jump, but the perfect judgment.

HELLO, BEN. GUESS WHO I JUST MET WITH? YOUR OLD FRIEND DICK GRAYSON.

YEP. WE WERE JUST TALKING ABOUT YOU! ISN'T THAT *FUNNY?*

LEEEEAASEEEE. LEASSSSE...

NOW, WHERE WERE WE?

HUNGRY CITY
PART THREE OF THREE
SCOTT SNYDER: WRITER   JOCK: ARTIST & COVER
DAVID BARON: COLORS   SAL CIPRIANO: LETTERS

SKELETON KEY

SCOTT SNYDER

FRANCESCO FRANCAVILLA

HOW, THOUGH? WHAT'S HIS PLAN?

WELL, HE CAN'T JUST TOSS THE STUFF INTO THE RESERVOIR. IT'LL GET CLEANED OUT AT THE TREATMENT PLANT.

BESIDES-- AND HERE'S THE GOOD NEWS--LUCKILY, THE POTENCY IN THE FORMULA HE'S MADE, IT'S RELATIVELY LOW... I'M NOT SURE THAT IT'D HAVE A TREMENDOUS EFFECT ON THE *ADULT BRAIN* ANYWAY.

MAYBE ON CHILDREN, BUT STILL...

OH NO...

WHAT IS IT?

LESLIE. SHE SAID HE'D VOLUNTEERED TO DO *NUTRITION RUNS* FOR THEM.

WHAT ARE NUTRITION RUNS?

ONE OF LESLIE'S CLINIC'S MAIN FUNCTIONS IS THE DISTRIBUTION OF NUTRITION *FOR INFANTS.*

BABY FORMULA. GOTHAM BLOSSOM FORMULA COMPANY. THEY GIVE THE CLINIC FREE SUPPLIES OF FORMULA.

ON A NUTRITION RUN, SOMEONE GOES TO THE PLANT AND PICKS UP CASES OF BABY FORMULA.

THEY GO TO THE PLANT?

INSIDE THE PLANT. WHERE THE VATS ARE. INSIDE! HE'S PLANNING ON GIVING THIS *POISON TO GOTHAM'S CHILDREN!*

JIM?

JIM, SOMETHING'S COME UP.

Gotham. It's a city of glass and concrete, of steel and brick.

And yet for me, like most people here, there's a city **beneath** the one I can see and smell and feel below my tires right now.

A city of memory. With a geography that only **I** know.

Where the biggest buildings, the most important landmarks, are the ones where something happened to **me**. Some tragic bulletin. A first kiss.

And after all these years, my city, the one beneath the glass and steel, is full of plenty of bright streets and dark alleys.

But the darkest spots on the map, the looming black towers, were almost all created by one man--**the Joker.**

In many ways, he's Gotham's darkest and most brilliant architect.

And to be honest, right now, at this moment, I'm terrified of what he has built for **me**.

KANE SQUARE HOTEL, HOW MAY I DIRECT--

CAN YOU CONNECT ME WITH *BARBARA GORDON,* PLEASE? ROOM 639. IT'S *URGENT.*

MAY I--

TELL HER IT'S *JIM.*

HELLO?

BARBARA, IT'S ME!

JIM? WHAT'S WRONG?

THE JOKER, BARBARA. HE'S *OUT.* LISTEN, I'M SURE I'M JUST BEING OVERLY CAUTIOUS, BUT I CALLED HOTEL SECURITY AND--

THE JOKER? I DON'T UNDERSTAND. YOU THINK HE'D COME AFTER ME? WHY?

I DON'T KNOW. BECAUSE THAT'S WHO HE *IS,* BARB. HE ALWAYS COMES AFTER US, OUR FAMILY. ANYONE I CARE ABOUT. LIKE I SAID, THESE ARE JUST PRECAUTIONS, BUT *PLEASE,* JUST STAY IN THE ROOM 'TIL I ARRIVE.

BUT HOW COULD HE KNOW WHERE--

BECAUSE HE ALWAYS KNOWS, DAMMIT!

PLEASE, BARB, I'M LIKELY WRONG, BUT YOU NEED TO PROTECT YOURSELF JUST IN CASE! NOW WHEN HOTEL SECURITY--

KNOCK KNOCK

WAIT, JIM? THEY'RE AT THE DOOR NOW. HOLD ON.

GOOD. JUST GO WITH THEM, BARBARA...

I'M PULLING UP DOWN-STAIRS NOW.

YES? WHO IS--

CRASH

>SIGH< WE'RE GOING TO HAVE TO PUT THAT BASTARD IN A *BUBBLE*, AREN'T WE? A REAL BUBBLE. IT'S GETTING--

HOLD ON, DETECTIVE BULLOCK.

YES?

WE RAN DIAGNOSTICS ON THE TOXIN AND FOUND SOMETHING STRANGE.

JOKER HAS USED MORE THAN *FIFTY* DIFFERENT VERSIONS OF THE TOXIN--THAT WE *KNOW* OF.

THE ONE HE USED ON HIMSELF AND ON BARBARA SR. IS ACTUALLY ONE OF THE *OLDEST* FORMS.

THE TOXICITY, THOUGH. HE NEEDED TO TAKE SOMETHING SO POTENT THAT IT WOULD MAKE HIS OWN SWEAT DEADLY TO THE TOUCH.

THAT'S THE THING. THIS FORMULA IS ACTUALLY *LESS* DEADLY THAN MORE RECENT VERSIONS OF THE TOXIN.

IT WAS MIXED WITH A REFINED ALCOHOL TO FACILITATE EXCRETION THROUGH THE PORES.

AND BARBARA SR.?

RECOVERING, LUCKILY.

"THE COMMISSIONER IS DOWN THERE WITH HER NOW..."

"AND THE VISUALS ON JOKER?"

When I was a boy, my parents kept a **big map** of the country tacked to the wall of our dressing room.

The map had pins stuck in all the places our troupe was going to stop that season.

Different towns and cities were marked with different color pins.

Blue pins meant small towns...which meant small shows, less dangerous tricks.

Red pins meant big cities. So, big shows and more dangerous tricks.

All the stops were marked red or blue.

Except for one--**Gotham City**, which was marked by a **black pin**.

According to my father, the black pin meant **no holds barred**. Pull out all the stops. Bring down the house.

It meant put on the biggest, riskiest show of the season. No catch wires. No safety nets. Everyone pushing themselves to the limit.

WE'LL GET HIM, COMMISSIONER.

"YOU ALWAYS WENT AROUND WITH YOUR HEART ON YOUR SLEEVE. YOU WERE *GENUINELY* NICE--THAT WAS THE THING. IT WASN'T AN ACT. YOU CARED ABOUT EVERYONE.

"AND ME...I WAS *DIFFERENT.*

"OF COURSE, EVENTUALLY, LIKE ANY KID, I STOPPED WORRYING AND JUST *ACCEPTED* WHO I WAS.

"I LEARNED TO 'GO WITH IT,' I GUESS.

"LAST YEAR, THOUGH, WHILE I WAS IN TEXAS, I COULD FEEL THE LAW COMING. I FELT BARBARA LOOKING FOR ME, TOO...

"...SO WHEN I CAUGHT WIND OF A CLINICAL TRIAL FOR PEOPLE LIKE ME, A TRIAL THAT I COULD TUCK MYSELF AWAY IN FOR A LITTLE BIT, I ENROLLED."

POLICE 911

"AND TO BE HONEST, I WAS INTERESTED TO SEE IF THE MEDICATION WOULD WORK."

"FUNNY THING, THE MEDICATION, THE DIAXAMENE, *DID* WORK."

"I ACTUALLY FELT THINGS, FOR PEOPLE. NOT THE WAY YOU DO, BUT A LITTLE BIT--A PINCH OF *EMPATHY,* I GUESS.

"AND IT MADE ME REALIZE SOMETHING. SOMETHING *BIG.* WHAT I REALIZED WAS..."

"...EMPATHY, DICK-- EMPATHY IS THE GREATEST HUMAN *WEAKNESS.* IT'S A HANDICAP. A VESTIGIAL LIMB.

"I SUDDENLY SAW IT SO CLEARLY, THERE IN THAT REC ROOM. ALL THOSE YEARS, I'D THOUGHT SOMETHING WAS WRONG WITH *ME.*

THAT I WAS *DAMAGED...* BUT NOW I SAW THAT IT WAS EVERYONE *ELSE* THAT WAS WRONG IN THE HEAD...

"...EVERYONE ELSE WHO WAS DYSFUNCTIONAL. BUT MEN LIKE THE ONES IN THE STUDY WITH ME, MEN FREE OF COMPASSION--WE WERE THE *STRONG ONES,* THE MORE HIGHLY EVOLVED.

"I KNEW IT. I KNEW I WAS RIGHT. BUT EVEN SO, I DIDN'T KNOW HOW MUCH LONGER I COULD GO ON THE WAY I HAD BEFORE WITHOUT GETTING CAUGHT...SO I WAS AT A *CROSSROADS.*

"YOU COULD EVEN SAY I WAS LOST, UNTIL..."

"...GOTHAM CITY SENT ME A *SIGN.*

"A SIGN IN THE FORM OF A NEWS REPORT. A REPORT ON THE *RETURN OF BATMAN.*

GNN BREAKING NEWS: THE DARK KNIGHT RETU...

"THERE WAS THIS PICTURE OF HIM, OF *BATMAN,* AND HE WAS LEAPING DOWN ON CRIMINALS, BUT THE THING WAS, HE WAS...*SMILING.*

"AND ALL OF A SUDDEN I JUST KNEW. I KNEW THAT IT WAS YOU UNDER THE MASK.

"NOT BRUCE. *YOU.*

PATIENT NAME: GORDON, JAMES JR.

"AND IT ALL MADE SENSE AT THAT MOMENT. I KNEW WHAT I HAD TO DO.

"SO I PACKED MY THINGS. AND I CAME BACK TO GOTHAM."

"...HE'S ABOUT TO HAVE A GOTHAM MOMENT OF HIS OWN."

SEE? FREEDOM.

BLAM

COMMISSIONER.

ME, TOO. BUT WITH NO TAKERS FROM THE DEPARTMENT AFTER THIS LONG... I SUPPOSE THE IDEA WAS MORE *WISHFUL THINKING* THAN ANYTHING ELSE.

WELL, I'D BE REMISS IF I DIDN'T THANK YOU, DICK.

OF COURSE. IT WAS THE LEAST WE COULD DO, GIVEN--

NO.

I MEAN *THANK YOU.* ON ALL FRONTS.

YOU'RE WELCOME.

AND OUR LAST BIT OF BUSINESS?

RIGHT. WE RAN ANOTHER ANALYSIS ON ALL THE BABY FORMULA TYPES LEAVING THE PLANT THAT JAMES HAD ACCESS TO, BUT THE RESULTS WERE STILL INCONCLUSIVE.

LONG AGO ENOUGH FOR ANY REAL TRACE OF THE STUFF TO BE GONE FROM THE VATS AS THEY STAND NOW.

IF HE DID TAINT THE FORMULA WITH THAT DRUG HE COOKED UP BY BASICALLY INVERTING THE DIAXAMENE REACTION, HE DID IT *LONG AGO,* LIKE HE SAID.

SO WHETHER HE INFECTED HUNDREDS, MAYBE *THOUSANDS* OF INFANTS WITH A DRUG THAT COULD HELP THEM GROW UP TO BE SOCIOPATHS-- WHETHER OR NOT HE DID THAT, WE *DON'T KNOW?*

MY HONEST OPINION IS THAT IT'S UNLIKELY. THERE WOULD'VE BEEN GREATER RESIDUAL MATERIAL.

BUT IT'S POSSIBLE.

IT IS.

->SIGH<- THIS CITY...I'LL TELL YOU SOMETHING, DICK. SOMETIMES I WONDER WHAT KEEPS ME HERE. REALLY.

COMMISSIONER, THIS PAST YEAR, HERE IN GOTHAM, I'VE SEEN SOME OF THE MOST HORRIFIC THINGS IN MY LIFE.

THERE ARE TIMES IT ALMOST FEELS LIKE THE CITY KNOWS YOUR GREATEST FEARS, KNOWS--

YOUR *NIGHTMARES.* I KNOW.

AND HERE, TODAY, ALONE HERE IN THIS ROOM, I'LL TELL YOU THAT I THINK MAYBE THAT'S WHY I'VE AVOIDED PUTTING DOWN ROOTS HERE IN GOTHAM ALL THESE YEARS.

MAYBE DEEP DOWN, I KNEW HOW VICIOUS, HOW *CRUEL* THE CITY COULD BE.

THE THING IS, BEING HERE NOW, ON THE OTHER SIDE OF ALL THE *TERRIBLE* THINGS THAT HAPPENED THIS YEAR, I KNOW THAT THIS IS WHERE I *NEED* TO BE.

WHERE I *WANT* TO BE. BECAUSE I KNOW--LIKE YOU DO--THAT IF YOU MAKE IT THROUGH GOTHAM'S TRIALS, IF YOU CAN STAND UP TO THE MONSTERS IT THROWS AT YOU, YOU COME OUT REDEEMED. A STRONGER VERSION OF YOURSELF.

WELL, I FOR ONE HOPE YOU'LL STICK AROUND A WHILE THIS TIME, DICK.

I HAVE TO NOW. I'M STUCK WITH 4,000 FEET OF OFFICE SPACE I NEED TO CONVERT. I CAN'T IMAGINE SELLING IT'S GOING TO BE AN EASY FEAT.

the face in the glass

SCOTT SNYDER writer

JOCK & FRANCESCO FRANCAVILLA artists

DAVID BARON and FRANCESCO FRANCAVILLA colors

JARED K. FLETCHER letters

"SO WE'RE BOTH HERE FOR THE *LONG HAUL.*"

"I GUESS SO."

"WELL THEN, ALL THAT'S LEFT TO DO IS HANG OUR HATS, BELLY UP TO THE BAR, AND BE READY FOR WHAT COMES NEXT."

the end

Cover sketch for

DETECTIVE COMICS #871

by Jock

the black mirror

Cover sketch for DETECTIVE COMICS #872 by Jock

BAT IN
TEETH

2
INSIDE
FIGURE

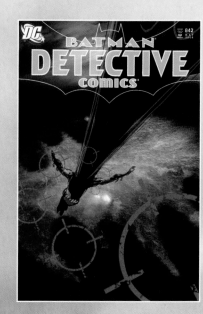

Cover sketches for

DETECTIVE COMICS #878 by Jock

Cover sketches for DETECTIVE COMICS #874 by Francesco Francavilla

Unused cover and sketches for DETECTIVE COMICS #874 by Francesco Francavilla

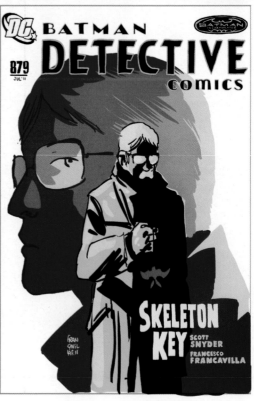

Cover sketches for DETECTIVE COMICS #874 & 879 by Francesco Francavilla

HE KNOWS ALREADY...
WHEN *SCOTT* TOLD (BATMAN EDITOR) *MIKE MARTS* THAT I WOULD HAVE BEEN PERFECT FOR TELLING THE JAMES JR. STORY, MIKE REPLIED HE WASN'T REALLY FAMILIAR WITH MY WORK.

I REALIZED SOME CONVINCING WAS NEEDED, SO I DREW THE STRIP BELOW WITH JIM GORDON, HARVEY, AND BATMAN, AND SENT IT TO MIKE.

AND THAT SEALED IT: I WAS ON BOARD THIS DETECTIVE RUN. I AM SO GLAD I DID THAT STRIP, SO SO GLAD. :)

F.F.

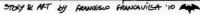

STORY & ART BY FRANCESCO FRANCAVILLA '10

LOBBY-CARD STYLE POSTER I DID FOR **SKELETON CASES** THAT WAS USED IN EARLY P.R. ON **DC COMICS'** OFFICIAL BLOG, **THE SOURCE**.

Detective
COMICS
#871

SKELETON CASES

JAMES JR. character design

1

2

FRAN
CAVIL
LA F.10

FRAN
CAVIL
LA F.10

FRAN
CAVIL
LA F.10

3

FIGURES 1 & 2 WERE THE INITIAL CHARACTER DESIGNS FOR *JAMES JUNIOR.* WE ALL AGREED WE WANTED JR. TO BE MORE *"GENERIC,"* THE KIND OF PERSON YOU WOULD SEE WALKING DOWN THE STREET OR ON THE METRO AND WOULDN'T EVEN NOTICE HIM. SO I WENT BACK TO THE DRAWING BOARD AND CAME BACK WITH THE VERSION IN *FIGURE 3.*

I ALSO DECIDED TO GIVE HIM GLASSES FOR 2 REASONS: **A)** THEY HELP TO MAKE JR. LOOK LESS DANGEROUS AND A LITTLE UNSETTLING AT THE SAME TIME. **B)** PLAYING ON SCOTT'S BLACK MIRROR THEME, I WANTED HIM TO HAVE GLASSES LIKE HIS DAD, SORT OF A DARK REFLECTION OF GOTHAM'S FINEST COP.

AND THUS JAMES JR. WAS (RE)BORN!

Page developments by Francesco Francavilla

PENCILLER FRANCESCO FRANCAVILLA F.F.
TITLE DETECTIVE COMICS - IN THE BLOOD
ISSUE # 874 MONTH JUL-11
PAGE # 17-18 INTERIORS

FRANCESCO FRANCAVILLA F.F.
DETECTIVE COMICS "THE FACE IN THE GLASS"
88? 10-11 AUG-11

The following is the first-draft script by Scott Snyder for SKELETON CASES PART ONE that appeared as the backup feature in DETECTIVE COMICS #871. Seen in this collection on pages 82-89. This story is the introduction of James Jr.

DETECTIVE #871 · PAGE 23

23.1
CLOSE on a TRENCH COAT hanging in a closet, among a couple simple jackets and old police uniforms.
This trench coat is JIM GORDON'S iconic jacket. We're inside Gordon's apartment, and it's late at night, FF.

> GORDON CAPTION: "These are the questions I get asked the most by people around Gotham…"

> GORDON CAPTION: "And these are my answers."

23.2
CLOSE on a FRAMED DET OF 5 BADGES, showing Gordon's progression from an officer in Chicago to commissioner in Gotham:

BADGE 1: POLICE OFFICER: CHICAGO DEPT. OF POLICE.

BADGE 2: DETECTIVE: CHICAGO DEPT. OF POLICE.

BADGE 3: LIEUTENANT: GOTHAM CITY POLICE DEPT.

BADGE 4: CAPTAIN: GOTHAM CITY POLICE DEPT.

BADGE 5: COMMISSIONER: GOTHAM CITY POLICE DEPT.

The inscription at the bottom of the framed mementos: *"Happy Father's Day to an Unlawfully Great Dad, Love, Babs."*

> GORDON CAPTION: "'You ever shot anyone?' And my answer is, 'Too many times.'"

> GORDON CAPTION: "'You ever been shot?' And my answer is, 'Too many times.'"

> GORDON CAPTION: "And the question I get the most… 'How do you leave it all behind when you go home?' My answer to this one is: 'You learn to block it out.'"

23.3
CLOSE on a set of FRAMED ARTICLES from the Gazette, and others, showing Gordon triumphant at the end of notable cases. One article could be by Vicki Vale.

HEADLINE 1: Clown Prince's Plot to Poison Reservoir Foiled by Intrepid Police Lieutenant.

HEADLINE 2: Police Department's War on Organized Crime a Success: Maroni and Falcone Families in Shambles After Series of Bold Convictions.

> GORDON CAPTION: "But that's not the truth."

GORDON CAPTION: "The real truth is that when you've been doing this as long as I have – you don't leave it behind. You can't."

> SFX (TELEPHONE – OFF PANEL): RING…. RING….

23.4
CLOSE on 3 FRAMED PHOTOS OF THE GORDON FAMILY on a shelf. The photos move backwards through time, left to right.

PHOTO 1: Gordon and Barbara, recently. He's standing behind her chair. They're posing together, smiling on a sunny day.

PHOTO 2: Gordon (back when his hair was red), Sarah Essen and a young, teenaged Barbara, smiling for the camera at the zoo.

PHOTO 3: This photo is set back from the others, notably in the shadows. Almost as though Gordon isn't sure to keep it up on the shelf anymore. It shows an even earlier scene – Gordon as a young man, hair bright red, holding a BABY BOY in his arms – like a 1-year-old, just old enough to see that this is a boy. This is JAMES JR. (Gordon's son, from continuity, as in Year One). We will see more of him soon... Barbara stands beside the two, a cute little girl, about 4 years old.

[NOTE: The continuity is conventional canon: Gordon was married to Barbara Sr. early on in his career, from Chicago to Gotham. They had James Jr. in Gotham. Jim's niece, Babs, sometimes visited (hence the early picture). After the divorce, James Jr. went with Barbara, and Jim eventually married Sarah Essen. The two of them adopted Babs as their daughter when she was a young teen. Nothing new.]

> GORDON CAPTION: "Because no matter how good you think you are at drawing a line between work and home, there will always be some cases that stay with you..."

> GORDON CAPTION: "Cases that come howling back at you out of the darkness, like phone calls in the middle of the night."

> SFX: RING... RING...

DETECTIVE #871 · PAGE 24
24.1
We're inside Gordon's bedroom now. JIM GORDON is sitting in bed, his back to us, holding the phone to his ear. Gordon is in his undershirt and boxers. This is a war-wagon of a man – still solid and strong, imposing, but also weathered, shoulders worn down by time.

> SFX: RIN-

> GORDON: Gordon.

24.2
Small – We're at the other end of the line with HARVEY BULLOCK. He's standing in the GOTHAM AVIARY. But this isn't important to show here, unless you do a touch or hint of feathers behind cage bars or something.

> BULLOCK: It's Harvey. I'm at the Aviary.

24.3
Gordon, standing, turning on the lights.

> BULLOCK (THROUGH PHONE): I got something you should see.

> GORDON: I'm listening.

24.4
Small – on BULLOCK, as he cradles the phone a bit, almost like he's trying to keep the call secret.

> BULLOCK: Jim, I think it's something *you should see*. For yourself?

24.5
Gordon standing before his closet, with the trench coat inside, reaching for the coat.

> GORDON: (sigh) I'll be there in fifteen.

DETECTIVE #871 · PAGE 25
25.1
Large – Gordon being led by Bullock into the GOTHAM AVIARY, a zoo for the world's most exotic birds. Most of which are now returned to their cages. It's late at night, and a COUPLE OF WORKERS are sweeping up, maybe closing the doors to a cage or two, now that the birds are mostly back. These are things that can be happening in the background of the following panels, as Gordon and Bullock walk to the main office. Touches occurring in the background. Take whatever liberties you want, too, FF! If you think focusing on the birds or cages for a panel or two would be effective – keeping Gordon and Bullock in the background, the workers/birds in the foreground I'm fine with it. Or, if you'd rather focus on Gordon and Bullock walking, keep the birds and aviary activity in the back, fine. The feeling should be tribal and creepy, animalistic – Gotham is changing, becoming more hungry and vicious and adapting to challenge Dick Grayson and Jim Gordon both.

> BULLOCK: So sometime around six in the evening, just after closing, the cages in the aviary sleeping quarters unlocked.

25.2

Bullock leading Gordon past the cages. Gordon is tired, could be rubbing his eye or something.

BULLOCK: Now Mayor Hady, he's all hot and bothered, see, because he has these dignitaries from some God-forsaken desert hole visiting Gotham this week and what's their first stop?

GORDON: The aviary. Harvey… It's late. I get the politics, but we got a felony "cruelty to animals" at best here.

25.3

Bullock, still leading Gordon past the cages.

BULLOCK: Just listen.

BULLOCK: The cages in this place are all automated. They're controlled by the aviary's main computer system.

DETECTIVE #871 · PAGE 26

26.1

Large - They enter a control room. There's an OFFICER manning the station. It's all surveillance – screens showing various parts of the aviary.

BULLOCK: Which means some time before closing, our guy snuck into the control room unnoticed, reprogrammed the cages, and set all the birds free-willy to flap around Gotham.

BULLOCK (TO THE OFFICER): A little privacy, pal?

OFFICER (DAN): Sure thing. Evening, Commissioner.

GORDON: Dan.

26.2

The guard leaving in the background as the two cops watch the footage in the fore.

BULLOCK: So Hady, he sends me and my guys down here to look over the surveillance footage.

BULLOCK: See if we spy anyone suspicious coming out of the aviary toward the end of the day. Choice assignment, right?

26.3

CLOSE on a SCREEN (grainy security monochromatic footage) showing a man walking out of aviary. If you want to show Harvey's hand in the panel, pointing, that's fine. The footage here should look like surveillance footage shot from a camera mounted above the exit gates of the main hall. So the angle should be high, looking down at people moving out of the hall, toward the exits. Among the people moving is a MAN, moving slowly. Taking his time. He is a plain-looking person, really. Slim, average height. Pants and a light jacket. Hair parted to the side (his hair is brownish red, though we can't see that here).

BULLOCK (OFF-PANEL): Anyway, I'm looking through the last hour of tape, barely paying attention, until I notice this guy exiting the main hall real late, right at closing.

26.4

Small - CLOSE on Gordon's face – he looks stunned, mouth open just slightly, eyes narrowed. Bullock is watching him.

BULLOCK (OFF-PANEL): You're seeing who I'm seeing, Jim?

26.5

Small - CLOSER on the MAN. He has paused. People are walking past him in a blur. But he's standing still. He is now beginning to look up at the camera.

BULLOCK (OFF-PANEL): Jim?

26.6

Small - EXTREMELY CLOSE on the man, who's now looking at the camera, smiling very, very slightly. This is JAMES JR., Jim Gordon's troubled son. He should look like a young version of Gordon, late 20s, but without the mustache. A nice-looking, trim, clean-cut man with glasses (maybe) and a slight, kind smile.

He should be wearing plain clothes. He dresses a little preppy, but casual. Khakis, a wind-breaker, a plain button-down beneath. Not cool. He's the kind of guy you wouldn't notice. He blends into the crowd. Get close to him, and there's something just a little creepy about his smile, something cold and vapid. Like he only smiles with his mouth, while his eyes keep the same calm, but alert stare all the time. In fact, I think it might be good to draw his eyes –which are a clear, light blue – with pupils that are always very contracted – tiny pinpoints of black (black pins, like the reference in the opening captions of the feature...). He looks like a nice young man, with something maybe just a tiny bit off about him, a little too intense...

[NOTE: Francesco – this is the star of your story. We're going to make him one of the scariest mothers in the DCU. The idea is that he is a true psychopath – devoid of empathy. He's been away for a long time, wandering, staying away. No one knows where he has been, but his last encounter with Jim was bad – years ago. Jim has always known something was "wrong" with him, but how wrong is a mystery to him. That's the idea: James Jr. is the worst thing Jim could have for a son – an unsolvable mystery. Jim cannot figure out what Babs (one of the very smartest in the Bat-family) knows instinctually – that James isn't just someone with an anti-social personality disorder. He's a killer. A true psychopath. For Jim, the evidence is never there, and even the reason for James' nature is a mystery to him. Was it the fall from the bridge that damaged him? Was it the fact that Jim worked long hours, and wasn't around? Was he just born that way? Or was it... Gotham? James is the twisted, mirror reflection of Dick and Jim, in that Dick is all about empathy and compassion; James has neither. Jim is all about solving things; James is unsolvable... Let's have some fun.]

       BULLOCK (OFF-PANEL): Jim...

DETECTIVE #871 · PAGE 27
27.1
An establishing shot of Gordon's apartment. It's still night – raining now.

       BULLOCK CAPTION: "You want me to put the word out, Jim? Just in case?"

       GORDON CAPTION: "Thanks, Harvey, no..."

27.2
Gordon, having just opened the door to his place, is now turning on the light.

       GORDON CAPTION: "That footage is rough as gravel. You'd be putting the word out on a ghost."

27.3
Small - CLOSE on his shocked face.

27.4
Because on the floor is a bright TRAIL OF BLOOD... leading toward the window, which is in the back-ground. If the window is visible here, there should be a dark SILHOUETTE on the shade, that resembles the shape of a man – like a man is standing outside Gordon's apartment, on the fire escape.

27.5
Larger – Focus on the window, as Gordon approaches. There's more blood on the sill, dripping down the wall beneath, as though someone dragged a bleeding thing to the sill and took it out onto the fire escape. And again, visible on the WINDOW SHADE IS A SILHOUETTE – it appears someone is standing on the fire escape.

       GORDON: Who's here?!

DETECTIVE #871 · PAGE 28
28.1
Gordon, coming toward us, approaching the window, GUN drawn.

       GORDON: Show yourself!

       GORDON: James?

28.2
Reverse: Gordon's POV as he approaches the window. His hand should be reaching for the shade...

       GORDON: James?

28.3
A mirror image of Gordon's hand reaching, his POV... But this time it's reaching for the handle of a boy's bedroom door. This is 15 years ago, a flashback, but should be an identical image to the one above. Visible through the crack, a young boy, 7 years old, in his pajamas, his back to us, playing with something we can't see. But there is blood on the floor...

        GORDON: James...

28.4
CLOSER on his hand reaching for the shade now.

        GORDON: James, what have you done?

28.5
Same image, but this time his hand is reaching for the little boy's shoulder. We still can't see what's on the floor, but we can see more blood... as though the boy is playing with something dead.

        GORDON CAPTION: "What have you done?"

28.6
Small - EXTREMELY CLOSE on Gordon's hand at the shade.

        GORDON CAPTION: "What have you done?"

28.7
Small – same image as the boy's face begins to turn towards us... Just a hint of his face.

        GORDON CAPTION: "What have you done?"

DETECTIVE #871 · PAGE 29
29.1
SPLASH –SCREECH! The shade is up – a big shot of a HARPY EAGLE SHRIEKING at us from the other side of Gordon's window. The giant ugly bird has a dead rat in its claws, bleeding onto Gordon's fire escape. In the foreground, Gordon recoils from the predatory bird.

DETECTIVE #871 · PAGE 30
30.1
We're outside, on the fire escape, the bird flying towards us as Gordon yells at it.

        GORDON: Go on! Get the hell out of here!

30.2
We're inside with Gordon as he shuts his window.

30.3
We're outside again, looking through the window at Gordon with a hand on his forehead, massaging his brow as he tries to calm down.

30.4
We're on the street, looking up at Gordon's window. And in the fore, a figure with his back to us.

30.5
Reverse: we're looking down a bit from a slightly high angle, at JAMES JR. He's looking up at his father. His face shows nothing maniacal or evil. Just strangely cold.

CREDITS:
"Skeleton Cases: Part One of Three"
Francesco Francavilla · artist
Scott Snyder · writer

T